Joy Trickles In

Navigating With Hope

A collection of poetry by
ULLIE-KAYE

changed.

yes, i have changed. you may not recognize
me anymore. the new me does not pretend to
be anything other than who i really am.
you may not recognize the kind of strength
that courses through my veins. it is rich
with suffering. and believing. and overcoming.
i no longer crave the things that i thought
made me beautiful. but rather, i am delicious
now in spirit. in choosing tenderness. and
deliberate breaths. and a longing to be to
others what i always wished for them to be
to me. i no longer have eyes that search for
approval. but my vision is on whatever brings
grace and healing and growth. i am full of love.
and empty of being consumed by things that
really do not matter. don't get me wrong. i am
still filled with a thousand, broken pieces -
i've just rearranged them all.

ullie-kaye

1

simplicity.

i am all day breakfast. cool breezes.
and bonfires past midnight. i am camp
songs. and church songs. and love songs
that remind me of country roads and
city lights and a heaven that is still
out there, waiting for me. i am tired
bones but hopeful mornings. i am grocery
store line conversations with cashiers.
and strangers. and people who just need
a new face to talk to. i am small acts of
kindness. and small steps of bravery. and
small ways to move mountains, one stone
at a time. i live for simplicity in a world
that likes to overcomplicate everything.
i am determined to heal. and determined
to grow. and determined to follow this path
to the bitter end — even when it gets hard.
these are the things that feed my soul.

ullie-kaye

mighty.

healing is hard.
whether physical, emotional or
spiritual, it is a profound life
experience. we are capable of so
much more than we give ourselves
credit for. the secret is finding
the balance between prioritizing
self, while preserving and
nurturing our relationships with
others. the irony is that as we
shift our focus to the light we
often need to go back to revisit
the darkness. the difficult part
is honoring those who want to help
while going much of it alone.
it is both working harder than
we ever have before and resting
harder than we ever have before.
it is eyes inward. and eyes upward.
it is trying. and trying. and trying
again. healing is hard. but the
healer is mighty.

ullie-kaye

fragments.

i guess it all comes down to this.
i have won some and i have lost some.
dearly lost some. and to this day,
my body aches because of things
that i just could not shake myself
loose from. i am not invincible.
my strength does not come by means
of powerful and blatant outward
expressions. in fact, i am at the
constant mercy of the very next
moment. i cling to fragments.
i grasp for small pieces of sunlight.
wherever and whenever and however
they come. i listen for whispers
of hope. those tender breezes that
tell me i am still able. and on my
best days, i believe them. i live in
the seconds of time that remind me
that i am a beautiful part of something
so much bigger. than here. and this.
and now. it is the only way i know.

ullie-kaye

wildly.

may we live each day in such a way
that fear itself is afraid to haunt us.
may we run wildly but always towards
those slivers and cracks of light that
illuminate the darkness. may we cheer
each other on because God only knows
how much we all need it. may we never
sink so low that we do not recognize
our own spirit. may we choose wisdom
and tenderness over careless words.
heartfelt emotion over empty gestures.
quiet giving over loud acts of charity.
may we rather forgive too often than
not enough. may we always strive to
find beauty. even if we must squint our
eyes and tilt our heads to see it.

ullie-kaye

5

moments.

i live for the small moments.
those increments of time where
life reminds me how good it is
to be alive. to watch the sun
spill onto the sidewalk as though
she is telling me to keep moving
forward. to count my blessings,
not by the number of people who
have loved me but rather by how
great a love one single soul can
give. i am rich in knowing that
growth is painful. that pain is
essential. that time is of the
essence. and that somehow beauty
is found right there in the midst
of it all.

ullie-kaye

clover and mosses.

tell me again about
the way you endured.
how you took all the
things that were meant
to hurt you and planted
a garden. and how even
there, in the midst of
the clover and mosses,
you grew.

ullie-kaye

breathe.

sometimes when i cannot breathe, i turn
my lungs into rowboats and paddle as hard
as i can until i see land. i keep my eyes on
the shore and i do not let them blink.
not for even a minute, or i begin to sink.
sometimes when i cannot breathe, i make
a parachute from all of the things i have
overcome. i fill up my chest with air and i
remember to pull on my lifeline. i float down
softly until my feet hit earth and i am safe
again. sometimes when i cannot breathe,
i pretend that i am in a wide, open space.
a garden. a field. a forest. the river's edge.
and i inhale the splendor. i look up and out
and inside of myself and i notice just how
small i am against the greatness of nature.
i soak in the knowledge that i too, am full of
wonder. and wilderness. and waters that were
made for waging war. and so i worship instead.
sometimes when i cannot breathe, i imagine
doing somersaults or cartwheels or anything
that feels like absolute freedom. and i live
there for as long as it takes to shake the lie
that i will not survive. i will. and i can.
and i am stronger than i think.

ullie-kaye

i choose you.

love me wild-eyed or weary.
full of ocean and full of
dry land. half broken. and
half mending. quiet and
mysterious or spilling over
and telling you absolutely
everything. love me meek and
love me mighty. because sometimes
i am a boat, rocked to my core
by the storm. and sometimes
i am the storm. an avalanche.
a hurricane. and in advance,
i'm sorry. love me free and love
me bound to my downfalls but
trying. when light glistens
off my skin and when i stumble
into darkness. love me holy.
and sinful. and bleeding.
and healed. love me sweetly.
and softly. but tell me when
i have bruised your spirit.
in all of my life, i have found
no greater thing than to be
chosen. and so, with that,
i choose you, too.

ullie-kaye

be still.

be still and know. listen to the seas, they
tell you of overcoming. of understanding
when to be mighty and when to lay down
your tides to rest for awhile. to let yourself
feel. that sweet release of returning to wash
your tears at the brink of the shore. be still
and listen to the mountains. those skyscrapers
of endurance. heavy with ice laden peaks
and wind swept skin. how they yearn for love
despite their jagged edges. strength and
vulnerability merged. listen to the northern
lights. how they dance without rhythm. wildly
and brave. painting the sky in whatever way
their voices choose to bleed. in torrents of
color. smashing together and wandering apart.
yet how they soften sometimes to just the
faintest glow. a glimmer. a flicker of what they
once were. but still just as beautiful. listen to
the silence. it asks only for the absence of
distractions. to sit in oneness with God. your
heartbeat. your breath. the blinking of your
lashes as they meet halfway. finding peace.
to quiet the storms that have been raging for
longer than you had hoped. to trust the plan –
even when the plan does not align with yours.
be still and know.

ullie-kaye

contentment.

so let me then choose contentment.
to be astounded by all of the everyday,
mundane things. seawater. and bonfires.
and the twinkling of city lights. let me
soak myself in country roads that turn
and time that seems to stand still.
may i feel the breaths of every living
thing. the souls. the shores. the storms.
the stars, long gone but still glowing.
may i welcome tall grasses and wind-
swept trees. and may i never hurry
the pain, the path or the plan but rather
search for the purpose.

ullie-kaye

love leans in.

i have come to grasp this.
there are all kinds of people.
and each with their own set
of wounds and pasts and
ways of coping. one of the
hardest things i have had
to learn was that love leans
in despite our differences.
humans naturally respond
using their own set of broken
pieces. the things that they
have had to fight for. endure.
breathe through. and so, we
will often encounter those
who speak in a language that
we do not yet quite understand.
because the mother tongue of
pain can be so many things.
and in order to translate the
behavior, we must first know the
places from which they have
traveled.

                ullie-kaye

in the light.

i have become less afraid of spending
time in solitude. i have become more
comfortable with the fact that i will
always have parts of me that i dread.
that i will always be faced with darkness.
and self doubt. and all of the things
from days gone by that still attempt to
haunt me. and yes, i am prone to tripping
over the edges of my own shadow because
i will never be the epitome of graceful.
or perfect. or put together. but i am the
creator of this shadow and even more
beautifully, i was created. meticulously.
knit together. woven. stitched. full of
harvest some mornings and full of unsprouted
seeds, the next. sun that radiates from
every pore of my being and monsters that
won't let me go. i have told myself many
lies over the years but the truth is,
i cannot fear that which i embrace. and so,
i look myself in the eye and whatever it
is i see, i baptize it in love. i anoint it
in forgiveness. and i keep on walking in
the light like i'm alive.

ullie-kaye

right places.

i believe that everyone is sent into
our path for a reason. even the ones
who cross it only for a fraction of
time. even the ones who break us.
and leave us. or make us question
everything we ever thought we knew.
keep your head up, as tired as you are.
love is not supposed to hurt, sweet soul.
but growing does. and i know this beyond
a shadow of a doubt. even the wrong
people and the wrong choices can bring
us to the right places.

ullie-kaye

stepping stone.

if you stay kind even when the
world is not so inclined. if you
lead with your heart on the days
where it would be easier to make
war. if you forgive and forgive
often, including yourself. if you
let yourself feel the good, the bad
and the ugly and allow others in
to the 'unmade bed' parts of your
soul. if you see pain as a stepping
stone and learn from your mistakes.
if you walk the road less traveled.
if you run and grow weary. if you
fall. and fall. and fall again. but
still choose love. you have chosen
and you have chosen well.

ullie-kaye

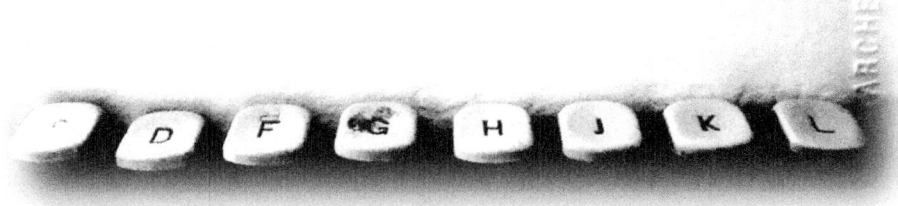

dear self.

dear self. do not listen to any voice
that tells you that you will not survive
this, including your own. show courage
in the smaller things and you will learn
that bravery does not always ask you to
leap into the wild unknown but rather
take one, single step forward – even if
you are trembling. go out of your way to
love in real and tangible ways. that is
not to say you must be elaborate. just be
authentic. show the world the less desirable
parts of you. and you will see the hurt
and broken ones lay their sorrow at your
feet a little more comfortably. acknowledge
your mistakes but do not dwell on them.
own them just enough to motivate change but
not so much that you become stuck in a
cycle of self pity or victimhood. when life
is hard, reach for the softer things.
forgive your shortcomings. fall into grace.
create a space that welcomes you.
free yourself from the guilt. and shame.
or anything else that makes a prisoner of
your ability to find peace. let yourself weep.
but just not forever. and above all else,
always look to the light. that's where the
healing comes.

ullie-kaye

16

then.

it is quite possible to become
a whole new person without
forgetting who you once were.
and it is quite possible to love
the one you have become, even
when the one you were, did not
love you then.

ullie-kaye

on fire.

go then and be beautiful in
all of the ways the world has
forgotten about. in the pages
of your authenticity. in the
breaststroke of your courage.
in the thunder of your overcoming.
in kindness. and love. and in
holding on when it would be
easier to let go. be the one that
they see and think to themselves,
"now there goes someone whose
soul is on fire."

ullie-kaye

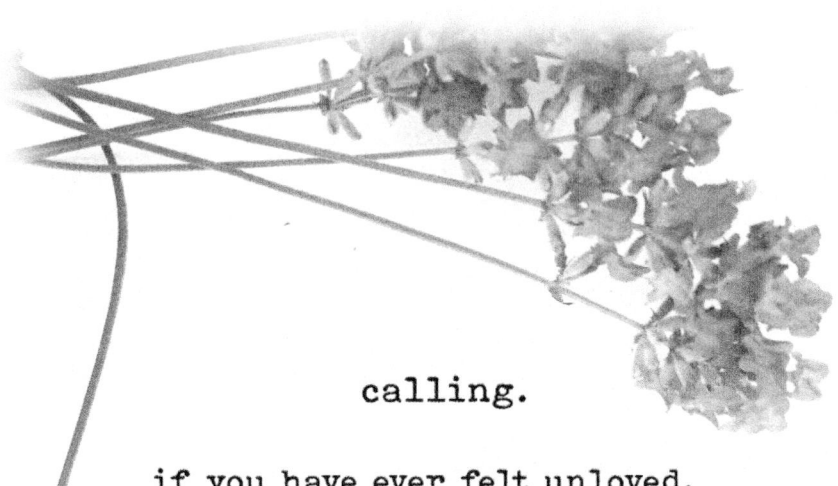

calling.

if you have ever felt unloved.
unseen. unheard. unknown.
i hope that you will spend the
rest of your life making sure
that no one else ever has to feel
that way. you have been there.
you know first-hand, the scars
it leaves. so go then and spill
your heart as wildly and vastly
as this earth allows. this is
your highest calling.

ullie-kaye

the process.

how did you heal?
- i didn't.
then how is it that you
can still face the sun
every morning like that?
- because i am healing.
but how do you know?
- because i'm finally okay
with not being healed
in the way that i wanted.
but choosing to know that
i AM being healed in all
the ways that i needed.
i am trusting the process.

ullie-kaye

20

alone.

i cannot emphasize this enough.
become comfortable with being in your
own presence. walk in nature. alone.
breathe in the wonder of silence. alone.
find a peculiar thing to invest your heart
and time into. alone. gather up a harvest
of cherished memories. alone. drink to all
of the beautiful things you have had the
honor of being a part of. alone. practice
tenderness. and joy. and creating a space
for peace. alone. solitude is such a powerful
way to come face to face with your own soul.
fall in love there, in these moments.
because sometimes you'll be the only thing
you've humanly got.

ullie-kaye

rare.

if you are that rare breed of human.
if you feel everything deeply because
you just cannot be indifferent. if you
have been broken but find strength in
overcoming. if you are full of chaos yet
deeply intuitive. if you know when to put
yourself last and when to make yourself
a priority. if you are afraid. but trying.
if your soul is caught in the pouring rain
and you still manage to find a piece of
solid ground to stand on. if the fire inside
you burns harder than all of the ones
that are simmering around you. do not let
the world change you. for the love of all
things holy, stay that way.

ullie-kaye

ordinary things.

i am in love with the ordinary things
of life. fresh air. acts of kindness.
old soul conversations. watching things
grow. listening to the rain as it empties
its heart towards earth. remembering
the times i ran through it. unafraid.
spontaneous. freedom-filled. i find
pure joy in the joy of others. i am drunk
on simplicity. and nostalgia. and old,
thrift shops run by volunteers who
just want to change the world one human
at a time. i greet the morning with eyes
that still have remnants of pain but will
see their way through it. i am determined
to create something beautiful every day.
whether art. or peace. or a path for those
who are lacking in light. i wish for nothing
more than soft hands filled with giving.
this is where i find my rest.

ullie-kaye

tomorrow.

i do not mind growing older. with age,
i have learned to weigh the things that
matter and the things that can be tossed
to the wind. i do not take lightly, the
ones who are sent into my path. whether
they carry with them, a load of suffering
or blazing beams of light, they partake
in my spiritual growth either way. i think
before i speak. i listen to my intuition.
i am not afraid to defend the truth.
even at the risk of being called crazy.
even at the risk of losing it all - it's all
or nothing anyway. i feed my soul.
because a well fed soul is a generous soul.
and i have come to know that the best way
to live is knowing it could all be gone
tomorrow. it could all be gone tomorrow.

ullie-kaye

who i am.

everything that i have learned on
this sacred earth. whether growth.
or healing. whether loving. or losing.
whether i fell gracefully into bliss
or stumbled madly into disaster.
whether i grew tired of trying.
or tired of all of the times i gave up
too easily. it is only because i swore
not to leave my own side. because i
looked at the one who carried my limbs
and said, "thank you". and because i
chose, even at the risk of being
misunderstood and unpopular, to march
to the beat of my own drum. even when
everyone walked away. that is the essence
of who i am.

ullie-kaye

make peace.

and if i may ask you
one thing, make peace
with it. whatever it is
that wakes you from
your sleep. whatever
it is that breaks you
into portions. whatever
it is that hunts you
like a thief and robs
you in broad daylight.
make peace. make peace.
make peace.

ullie-kaye

stay.

some friends will come and go.
some will remain tethered to your side
when they need you the most but wander
on to other pastures when life gets better.
some friends will have an instant soul
connection with you over a like-minded
endeavor. or path. or passion. and you
will radiate over how beautiful resonance
can be. some lifelong friends will never
reach the depths of you because there is
just too much of you to know. and other
friends will meet you for only a fraction
of time and have you spilling it all freely.
whether messy. magnificent. glorious. or grim.
and some friends will stay through it all.
through your mountains and valleys and
the breaths in between. they will stay.
but let me tell you this. every one of these
loves are precious. you will give sometimes
and grieve sometimes. you will win and lose
and find your way. this is the essence of
our human existence.

ullie-kaye

intense.

i am a gentle soul. i weep
at the sound that the rain
makes as it dances with the
pavement. i break when others
break. i am weak with awe at
the sight of a sunset. or the
twinkling of softened lights.
i am overcome by emotion at
the mere thought of suffering.
but i am intense too —
even fearless sometimes.
i do not hesitate to fight
battles. i am full of wilderness
and passion and scars that did
not come to grace this body
without tremendous sacrifice.
i do not let the world tell me
how to be. i am what i am.

ullie-kaye

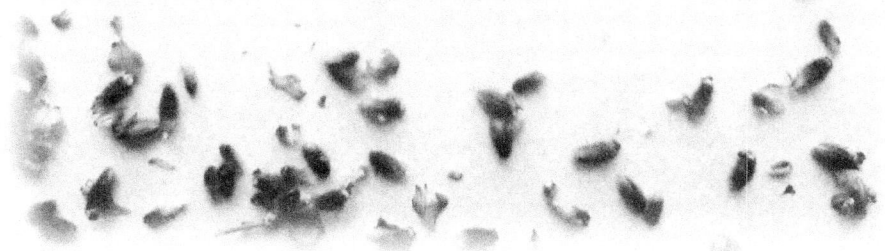

break free.

and if we are to heal. if we are to
live and love and build a fire within
our hearts again. if we want to be
revived. unearthed. resuscitated from
the past. the dark roads that nearly
had us believing that sorrow was a way
of life not just a temporary place to
stay. if we want to grasp at something.
light. hope. newness. fresh water. air.
a better way. we must learn the art of
breaking free. no more dwelling on
the things we cannot change. no more
hanging on to thoughts that inflict
wounds upon our own spirits. no more
settling for a flashlight because we
are undeserving of the moon. no more
pretending. or hiding. or measuring
ourselves against the magnificence of
others. let us run now, while we still
have an ounce of strength to loosen
the chains. if we are to heal, we must
break free.

ullie-kaye

woven in.

i crave solitude. those fragrant
mornings where there is nothing
standing between the sky and i.
but i crave connection too. there
are souls upon souls that live
inside of me. from every walk of
life. they're woven in. the ones i
cannot even remember never knowing.
and those strangers. those beautiful
strangers that cross my path for
only a moment but somehow still hum
their songs into the landscape of
my skin. i am richer for it all.

ullie-kaye

healing waters.

one of the most beautiful things on
this earth is watching broken people
walking alongside other broken people.
life is pain. it's true. but pain is growth
and growth is essential. so let us then
abide in love. let us stretch our arms.
and open our hearts. let us build bigger
tables. and fold ourselves into the
weariness of those who are lacking in
strength. let us become everything that
we ever wanted but never received.
let us walk in grace. and bring healing
waters. i can feel it. the light is near.

ullie-kaye

wisdom.

i am drawn to the older things
of this earth. buildings. bridges.
trees that have lived longer than
our minds can comprehend.
i am drawn to people who have
seen corners of life, i could only
imagine. those who have wandered
through hardship. and want. and
sacrificed everything. i am drawn
to old books. and old songs.
and old souls. and perhaps it is
wisdom that i seek. beautiful, time -
traveled wisdom. i can never quite
get enough of how she dances with
my spirit.

ullie-kaye

the path.

if you are in need of light, go to
the ones who have been through
the darkness. they will guide you.
if you are in need of hope, go to
the ones who have lost everything
and somehow still sing hallelujah.
they will show you the way. if you
are in need of strength, go to the
ones who have been down on their
knees, feeble and broken and weak
to the bone. they will know how to
gather up the courage to get back
up on fractured limbs and walk or
run or begin their freedom march.
if you need love, go to the ones who
have been without. who longed but
were forgotten. who sought but
were neglected. who dreamed but
were not given a chance. they will
understand the depths to which love
can save a soul. sometimes the path
to knowledge is simply in a human
whose shoes are worn but whose
heart is willing.

ullie-kaye

breakthrough.

i am an old and odd ocean of a soul.
filled with both vibrance and sadness.
with small pieces of goodness that i
try to leave on the path as breadcrumbs
for the others to follow. whatever love
and light i can muster. whatever storm
i can silence. whatever gifts i can bring
you. a place to fall freely and land
without judgment. to be honest, some days
i am just barely scraping by. these bones
weigh heavy. this heart has been injured.
but i live by this. i am more than the
accumulation of my pain - and so are you.
look for the dawn. sometimes our breaking
is really a breakthrough.

ullie-kaye

what is a soul.

i will not be lukewarm. i will not
dance half heartedly. i will not sing
with the windows rolled skyward.
i will not breathe a partial breath.
i will not hurt without feeling it all.
i will not love in fractions. and i will
not heal without a thousand miles
of work. of running madly. and wildly.
with sweat that pours profusely down
my face. i will not live without grace.
what is a soul, if not an earthquake,
rumbling.

ullie-kaye

beginning.

whatever you have been told. whatever you
have been taught to believe. whatever you
have had to fight for. walk through. be burned
at the stake for. whatever stars were stolen
from your eyes. whatever dreams were pulled
from underneath your feet. whatever madness
trampled you. whatever peace was stripped
from your body. i hope you showed yourself
grace. i hope you were tender with your own
spirit. i hope you had the capacity for a love
so big, it needed only for you to receive it.
i hope you found an inkling of worth and a
small burst of courage. i hope there was
sunlight. and music. and maybe some dancing.
and i hope too, that even when your most
beautiful things had to come to an end,
you were able to see a brand new beginning.

ullie-kaye

one.

one can be powerful.
getting through one more day.
taking one breath and then one more.
one person who believes in you.
one word that changes everything.
one step forward. one conversation.
one yes. one dream. one heart that opens -
ever so slowly but yet unfolding.
and in essence, are we not all made up
of many brave and beautiful one's?
one can be powerful.

ullie-kaye

37

angels.

you know when the wind blows just so.
when the sky lights up in mysterious
hues of gold and out of this world, blue.
when a song hits your deepest spaces at
precisely the moment your heart needed
to hear it. when a stranger smiles at you
and you walk on sensing you are somehow
fiercely known. when there is a burst
of beauty in the storm. when silence
beckons you with open arms and gives you
the safest place to fall. when you feel
a little braver. and a little more beautiful.
and a little more held.
it's because sometimes, angels.

ullie-kaye

good hearts.

we will lose the people that we love.
we will love the people who will never
know the depths to which we would
sacrifice it all for them. we will slay
beasts for people who would not slay
beasts for us. we will bring stars to
hands that are full of darkness and
light the fires of those who have become
weary of glowing. we will lose battles
we thought we would win and win battles
we thought we would lose. we will gain
strength in the most peculiar places.
we will stay as different as we were made
to be - even when it calls for us to walk
alone for awhile. but we will not grow
tired of kindness. that's what good
hearts do.

ullie-kaye

go.

are you tender? good. the world needs
more empaths. are you fierce? good.
the world needs more soldiers. are you
quiet? good. the world needs more of
those who ponder before they speak.
are you loud? good. the world needs
more activists on street corners.
and mountaintops. and thorn-filled
paths that require boots on the ground
and hands holding hands. are you broken?
good. the world needs those who understand
heartache. are you healed? good. the world
needs more stories from the ones who live
to tell the wonders. are you alive? good.
then dance. sing. heal. speak. create.
bless. listen. feel. give. bleed. go.

ullie-kaye

nourish.

i only realized how much i had
neglected myself, once i started
looking after myself.
grief takes a toll.
worry takes a toll.
loneliness takes a toll.
loving hard takes a toll.
even when that love comes from a
well meaning place. from a heart
that is golden. take the time to
nourish your soul. i beg you.
everyone is better off when you
can love with arms that are not
crumbling. and everyone is better
off when, with the same beautiful
devotion, you can love yourself too.

ullie-kaye

how beautiful.

i was born to be rebellious.
it is in my very nature to
ask questions, veer off the
beaten path and do things
my own way. i stumble around
until i find the meaningful
things in life. i prefer to
learn the hard way. i take
the long and scenic route home.
i take time to smell the roses
but i also take time to feel
the rain. sometimes i fall and
when i do, i usually fall hard.
i believe in making mistakes
and owning up to them. but i
also believe in forgiving
myself like i would anybody
else. life is full of crazy
and good and messy and mercy.
how beautiful.

ullie-kaye

each other.

may we never be so caught
up in our own lives that we
have a boat and do not offer
to pull them from the water.
and may we never say that we
were drowning and refused
the hand of a passerby.
hold onto this. in searching.
and sinking. and swimming.
and sighing.
we need each other.

ullie-kaye

time.

some things are most beautiful when
done slowly. a bonfire burning without
curfew. dreams that grow over years of
work and wilderness and wonder.
gardens that blossom without a hurry
in the world. waiting for warmth.
and rainfall. and softened soil.
a tender wandering amongst the wooded
groves; those tall oaks whispering their
words of wisdom. swaying in slow motion.
deep breaths made for comfort.
souls filled with journeys that can only
be measured in scars endured and wounds
that healed. but some things – some things
ask us to move with intention. to spill
freely. to forgive before they are gone.
to love them while we still can.
quick. time is not always on our side.

ullie-kaye

the potter.

you cannot break me.
you see, i have already been broken.
and in between the cracks that may
sometimes make me look fragile and
tender and lacking in might, i am held
together by the bones of mountains.
and victories. and every sharp turn
that i have ever had to take.
yes, i am merely clay. but that's okay.
the potter always knows a way to make
me sturdy.

ullie-kaye

roots.

so let me grow old then. let my grow roots
so deep that even when my blossoms do not
bloom, i am recognized by my steadfastness.
let me grow wild-eyed with forgiveness and
a thousand ways to love a sinner - of which
i too, am one. let my heart soften from
having known the harder things of life.
let it overflow with fullness from having
known the sound that emptiness makes when
it thunders in the valley and the shadows
of your lungs. let my bones become brittle
and my body fail me so that my spirit may
always burst and bubble and blaze above it.
and above all, let me fall. let me fall so
deep that i will never again see a soul that
is sinking and not reach for it with all
that is in me.

ullie-kaye

she.

you won't fit her into a box.
she doesn't do well with the
confines and shapes and
expectations of the world.
she knows the rules but would
rather write her own.
she is rebellious but only
in the name of revolution.
she thinks too much.
she dreams too much.
and she feels too much.
she is more wild than captured.
more crazy than sensible.
and more forgiveness than hurt.
she believes in loving. and living.
and setting things free. she is me.

ullie-kaye

beautiful mess.

and more than anything, i just
wanted to be true to everything
that i had inside of me. the gold.
the ashes. the blossoms. the deep,
wounded places. all of the things
that were swimming so perfectly
and disastrously through my veins.
to bring that beautiful mess beneath
my skin, to the surface and say,
"here i am, broken but willing.
what will you make of me?".

ullie-kaye

smooth sailing.

i asked for smooth sailing.
i was given a rowboat and
an ocean at high tide.
i asked for a compass to
find my way home. i was
given a map of all of the
places i had ever felt lost
but made my way through.
i had nothing that i wanted.
but everything i needed.

ullie-kaye

lighthouse.

i do not need my scars to fade.
i want them rather, to glimmer
brightly. to remind me for the
remainder of my days on earth
of the strength i was given in
some of my most tumultuous moments.
strength that i can only describe
as holy and unexpected and strangely
beautiful. i want them to shine
bravely enough to be a lighthouse
in the dark. so that when all of
the other lost and broken vessels
search for shelter, their hearts
look up and only see another soul
in need of grace.

ullie-kaye

known.

i think we all just want to be
known. not in the way of having
our names strung up in bright
lights or etched across the sky
in thunderous splendor. but to
truly feel like we matter. to know
that our absence makes someone
feel a little more empty and our
presence makes someone feel a
little more alive. we do not ask
for the stars but just want love
to pull up a blanket and watch
the stars beside us. it is the small
things, after all, that remind us
how great we are.

ullie-kaye

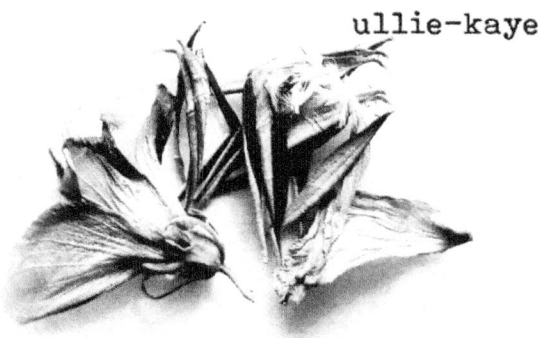

salt of the earth.

do you not know?
you are salt of the earth. you season
the tasteless things of the universe
and make them a little more heavenly.
you turn water into wine for the ones
whose faith in miracles has ruptured.
fallen. crashed and burned. where there
is pain, there you should be also. to walk
alongside. and carry the burden. to soak
up whatever tears are remaining. to love
the tender and wounded parts. the broken
hearts. you are the city on a hill.
there is a light in your eyes that was made
in the perfect image of someone else's
emptiness. i tell you the truth, even your
weaknesses can be used for strength in
those who have lost everything – use them
wisely. invite courage to live like stars
on the skies of every living being you
encounter. proclaim. and dance. and set
free the captive. and should you be the
captive one, look for the other salt of
the earth and city on a hill, people.
they are looking for you too.

                    ullie-kaye

authentic.

i am half lion. half lamb.
one part grace. and one part
fire. i run for shelter but
stare fear in the eye like it
does not own an ounce of
property on this sacred skin.
i am easily hurt. and easily
forgiving. i love too hard.
and break too hard. and laugh
too hard. and cry too hard.
but i consider it all good.
for not one piece of all this
gold, is counterfeit.

ullie-kaye

i would rather.

i would rather be the one who loves too
hard than not enough. who laughs too
loud than hide behind a closed mouth
grin. who rambles on about the universe.
the ache in my heart. or how the sound
of rain still reminds me of the time we
ran through it; skin drenched but happy.
i would rather learn the hard way.
take the narrow road. reminisce awhile
longer. stop to smell a flower in bloom.
i would rather grow wise with endurance
than give up and grow bitter. i would
rather aim high and know i tried than
shoot low and be praised for settling.
i would rather live a simple life than
a fabricated one. and may i always remember
this. my soul will only ever be as beautiful
as the lowliest person i've carried.

ullie-kaye

54

soul to soul.

i wonder what would happen if
we took a little extra time to
listen to someone else's story.
if we hugged a wounded warrior
until they collapsed so deeply
into our arms that we could feel
their pain unravel. i wonder
what would happen if we chose
our words with greater intention.
if we lifted each other up in
more soul to soul conversations.
i wonder what would happen if
we gave without expecting a single
thing in return. if we loved
simply because it was asked of us.
i wonder what would happen if
we chose peace over power.
built tables rather than walls.
bridges, rather than fences.
boats, rather than battlefields.
would there be more of us singing
than sinking?

ullie-kaye

ripple.

the most powerful thing is not
a storm. it is a ripple. storms grow
wild, wear wings like beasts and
then grow weak. a ripple builds
with soft hands. it believes in
the kind of strength that takes
time. that holds steady. that looks
for the small and the brave and
the beautiful ways to love.
it carries on without losing hope
in its potential. it lives in one,
single fraction of breath at a time.
a ripple changes everything.

ullie-kaye

up.

i am interested in the kind of people
who have walked a few miles on rugged
ground. who have felt the earth tremble
beneath their feet and somehow kept
on going. i am interested in the kind
of people who have lines around their
mouths and lines around their eyes and
a thousand years of wisdom, gleaned
from hardship and love and loss and
lacking. i am interested in the kind of
people who have had to fight for something.
who did not feel beautiful once but came
to understand that radiance is knit from
the strands of the soul within. i am
interested in the kind of people who
have had to hurt. and hope. and heal.
who learned the hard way. who chose
resilience. who never knew the kind of
strength that comes along when you have
nowhere else to look but - up.

ullie-kaye

breath of hope.

the thing is, we have a finite body
with an infinite soul. we are merely
humans with one foot on the earth
and the other one waiting for glory.
we build with our hands while
doing the quiet, steady work made
of light and healing and holiness.
there is only a small glimmer of time
that separates us from the realms
of space and distance as we have
come to understand them. herein lies
the breath of hope. to live a temporary
life with our eyes on the eternal.

ullie-kaye

survivor.

i am a survivor.
not because i am brave or fierce
or have moved mountains with my
bare hands. not because these ancient
stars still rise each night to give me
their standing ovation. but because
i have waged deep wars within.
quiet wars. unwelcome wars.
wars that took me by surprise
but did not win.

ullie-kaye

one million ways.

there are one million ways to change
the world. build a sanctuary for broken
things. or people. or creatures that fly.
or slither. or swim. or crawl. be a safe
place. a sounding board. a listening ear.
a shoulder to cry on. show them all of
the gold that is gleaming through their
cracks, then let them see your own slivers
too. take the stars and bundle them up
into your pockets so that on those days
where they need it the most, you can pull
them out like patio lanterns and light up
the sky. fireworks. firesides. fireflies.
be music to those who have never heard
words that sound like galaxies awakening.
like souls quaking. like love breaking
every barrier. every definition. and every
possibility. above all, if you really want
to change the world, be willing to look
inside the deepest chambers of your own,
small heart. that is, after all, where the
wonder begins.

ullie-kaye

comfort zones.

in your heart of hearts you
already know. do not question
the still, small voice that is
telling you which way to go.
you are afraid because things
will be different. feel different.
but then again, you are braver
now than you were back then.
and you have learned that strength
does not grow from comfort zones.
it grows from thorns. and high tides.
and wild, wild winds that knock
you off of your feet.

ullie-kaye

okay.

it's okay to have bad days.
it's okay to feel strong emotions
and weak to the bone. it's okay to
fall apart once in awhile.
it's okay to feel defeated. depleted.
incapable. and tired. and it's okay
to admit that you cannot do this
on your own. that you need a savior.
a healer. a shoulder. a good cry.
a miracle. a brand new beginning.
it's okay to find yourself in the
thickets of a thousand, wrong turns
and a thousand days where darkness
makes a dwelling place for you.
but go there only to visit awhile –
not to stay.

ullie-kaye

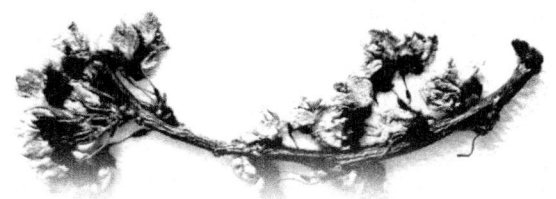

love is.

when you are with the people that you love,
grief is shared. pain is unburdened. joy is
multiplied. when you are with the people that
you love, you can see the beauty in the storm.
the light in the forest. the sky makes room
for both the stars that twinkle and stars that
fade and you know that you will be okay either
way. when you are with the people that you love,
you aim higher. you hold on tighter. you smile
bigger. you learn to open your heart up wide
and you are not afraid to let them inside.
when you are with the people that you love,
you hear the sound that hope makes when it
bounces off of words or laughter or heartbreak
that hurts but has an ever after. when you are
with the people that you love, the peace in your
soul outweighs the chaos. the sun rises every
morning to another day that was given but not
promised. when you are with the people that you
love, you understand that love is not to be
haphazard. it is not to be taken for granted
or expected in return. love is both the wildest
and the calmest thing of all.

ullie-kaye

lion and lamb.

the lamb in me says,
it is okay to be soft.
and sweet. and tender-
hearted. the lion in
me says, it is okay to
be fierce. and protective.
and even loud when it is
asked of me. and so,
i have chosen to be both.
how unapologetically
human of me to listen
to my calling. sometimes
i weep. sometimes i roar.

ullie-kaye

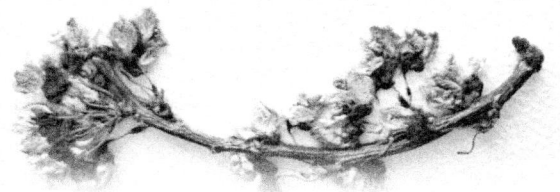

living water.

do not spend your time hunting for things
that pretend to make you happy but then
break into your ribcage at night and rob
your heart of peace. and sleep. and authenticity.
do not build pedestals for people who have
you believing that they are somehow better
for being shiny on the outside. your blood
is rich with gifts made of diamonds and rivers
and golden sunsets. use them. do not keep
yourself from learning. life is an encyclopedia
of pain and joy. every last word has the potential
of bringing you wisdom and light and closer to
grace. do not waste them. do not listen to a
world that gives you directions on a road they
have never traveled. listen rather to the stirring
of the wind-mingled fire that burns inside your
lungs and speaks in whispers that are stronger
than silence but softer than a warm embrace.
it's called conviction. do not drink water from
the runoff. you are worth so much more than
just the remnants. go to the fresh springs and
the mountaintops and the fountains flowing
freely. there is living water all around you and it
never runs dry. it will satisfy your soul, i promise
you. and do not waste a single opportunity to
love someone who has yet to decode its mysteries.
be the reason they wake up and look up and
breathe in color again. do not spend your time
hunting for things that pretend to make you
happy.

ullie-kaye

wildflowers.

i do not need oceans of people
by my side. even too much beauty
can overwhelm me. but let me ask,
if i may, for just a few, small
wildflowers on my way. those free
and imperfect scattered souls.
those mighty and steadfast champions
of light. ever growing. and flowing.
and blowing. and glowing. beside me.

ullie-kaye

tug of war.

isn't it insane to know how the things
that can hurt us so deeply can also be
the same things that make our souls
rich with overcoming? in a way, i think
we are in a constant push and pull
between wanting what we want because
it feels good and wanting what we need
because there is no greater thing on earth
than to say, "i have made it" (but only
because i surrendered it all). and "i am
strong" (but only because i did not rely
on myself). it's ironic, i know. and maybe
it's because i understand the desire for
calm as much as i do, the need for the
tempest. how it swirls and roars in my
innermost being. how it rearranges pieces
of my heart that i never even knew needed
rearranging. but they did. oh they did.
and so i beg to be surrounded and i beg
to be alone. and there are no less than a
thousand contradictions inside me at any
given time. you see, i am learning the ways
of the river. how it swerves and bends and
somehow stays in formation. a path forged
between rocks and flowing waters.
a tug of war that has me building walls
and laying myself bare. and that running
away from myself will never really get me
anywhere.

                    ullie-kaye

67

the view.

everything will start making
a lot more sense once you are
standing on the other side of
the valley and see the view.
but how beautiful a thing it is
to sit in the depths of the deepest
dark and know nothing at all
of what is to come and still hold
out your hands as though you are
welcoming splendor.

ullie-kaye

i hope love finds you.

i hope love finds you.
i hope love finds you and reaches itself
around your insecurities and builds you
mountains with its own bare hands.
i hope you wake up every morning to music
that makes you weep. or remember.
or stand a little braver. i hope you listen
when they tell you stories of how you made
them feel like everything. or how you would
have emptied the sky of all but a thousand
stars and the larks that grace the ears and
eyes of the lonely. that you carried a lantern
like it was the only thing that ever really
mattered. i hope love finds you sheltered.
and held. and a little bit broken but okay.
and when you sit at last on your weary bed
and long for yesterday, i hope love finds you
there too. always searching. always worthy.
and always in the presence of angels.

ullie-kaye

69

spirit.

you cannot break my spirit.
i will take your anger and build a fire
to keep warm the ones who have lost too
much. or loved too hard. or felt the weight
of things that should never have been theirs
to hold. i will take your silences and string
together sentences filled with "i love yous"
for all of those who have never been anointed
in the words that sound like heaven to their
senses. i will take the war dripping from
your fingertips and make an ocean filled
with nothing but a soft place to land.
because i refuse to let myself be a product
of anything that does not reflect inner peace.
and beauty and all of the mighty things that i,
by grace alone, have overcome.
no. you will not break my spirit.

ullie-kaye

70

do not become a hero.

do not become a hero.
become an earthly vessel, carrying a
hope that is nothing less than otherworldly.
become a servant. a giver. humble in spirit.
poor in self but rich in love.
do not become a hero.
become rather, one who opens the eyes of the
blind to the kind of sight that even the
mountains get down and beg on their knees for.
become a sinner who knows that when everything
else is stripped away, only grace remains.
then live by it.
do not become a hero.
do not save those who are drowning and then
wear your silver and gold upon your chest.
but choose to rest, knowing that your calling
is to scatter the truth. and plant the seeds.
and watch them grow – quietly.
do not become a hero.
forgive the ones who do not deserve it, then
remind yourself of why they do.
because you do too. (you do too).
build an altar out of suffering. let the winds
bring its incense to the heavens. ask how it can
teach you. lay down your sword. drink the fresh
water. be a beacon. always be a beacon.
but do not become a hero.

ullie-kaye

71

a quiet life.

there is something to be said about
leading a quiet life. i have tried to
fill these spaces with so many things.
the things i believed to be beautiful.
outward things. material things.
the need for validation. i have walked
on the wild side and i can tell you
right now, it will not quench your restless
spirit. but it was always in the silences.
the reflections. the solitude. those still
and grace-filled waters. the path of wisdom.
work. and pain. the unspoken realization
that i was exactly where and who i needed
to be - this broken vessel of a soul,
just learning how to love and let myself
be loved. nothing on earth can give you
that kind of peace. nothing.

ullie-kaye

wallflower.

i am an old soul with new found
courage. i am wise beyond my years
from pain and grief and mistakes
that i've made. but i will be the
first to tell you how much i have
yet to learn. i have, no doubt,
broken the hearts of those to whom
i could have shown more mercy.
but i have wounded my own heart
too. and sometimes i have even
wondered if it was beyond repair.
i am constantly working on myself
but i'm a far cry from perfect.
i am soft. but strong. i may not
have many by my side but for those
i do, i carry the things they have
told me in confidence, to my grave.
i do not mind being a wallflower
and fading into the background.
but there are days where i am
called to make waves. and i will
not hesitate to do so. i still hide
the parts of me that i am growing
to love. but i am growing to love
more of the parts of me that i have
always tried to hide.

ullie-kaye

73

constellations.

so then, may love kiss you softly
between the eyes. may you always
ache enough to know suffering but
hope enough to keep joy. may you
win more battles than you lose and
recognize that bravery is sometimes
just a quiet rumble in your chest.
may your pockets be filled with
a thousand, shimmering stars so that
even on your darkest nights, you can
string together constellations from
your very own emptinesses.
may kindness flow freely from every
pore of your skin, bleeding sunlight
onto those who have you convinced
that it would be easier to retaliate.
and on that morning when you wake up
to find you no longer believe in that
which holds your earth together,
may there be one more fighting breath
and one more breath again.

ullie-kaye

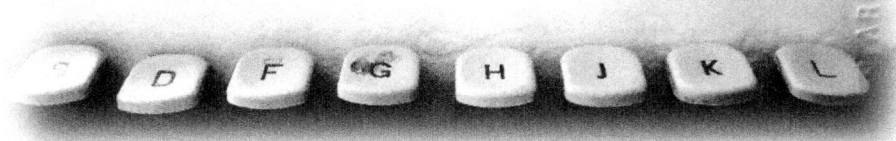

amazing grace.

the reason you are worthy is not
because of anything you have or
have not done. it is because you were
woven together. stitch by stitch.
detail by detail. and because your
body carries a soul that extends
much deeper than your skin. it is
because you have the ability to think
and feel and choose and love and believe.
to live with intention. to soak yourself
in both sunlight and rain and come
to understand that you need equal
portions of warmth and water to grow.
how beautiful to know that we are not
measured by what holds us captive
but rather by what sets us free –
amazing grace.

                    ullie-kaye

to do list.

bake bread. sit under a willow.
watch the stars. survive a storm.
find a second hand store and buy
something that reminds me of a
soul, long gone but never forgotten.
write a letter. old school. pen and
paper. send it. to myself. to God.
to someone who just needs to remember
why they still have breath inside
of their lungs. bury my regret.
plant a tree instead. carve my pain
into the sand then watch it wash away.
read about heaven. or ways to grow.
or an autobiography on someone who
changed the world for the better –
take notes. build a fire. stay warm.
look up. say "thank you". smile more.
remember how very precious i am.
be gentle on myself. find a mirror.
say, "i love you".

ullie-kaye

carry on.

until you understand that life was
not meant to be easy. or perpetually
beautiful. or without pain or risk
or loss. you will not know what miraculous
things you are made of. you will not
know to what extent your strength
can push you through and what it feels
like to build a bonfire inside of your
very own lungs that roars and billows
and fights to the bitter end. you will
not recognize the sound that tragedy
makes when it begins to sing hallelujah
into the vocal chords you believed to
this day, were fast asleep. and you will
never understand how capable you are
to sit in silence and listen to the voice
that says, "carry on, child, your work
is not yet done here."

ullie-kaye

live well.

everyone always hopes that they live long.
i just hope that i live well. i hope when i
reach the finish line, that i will be found
to have run the race the best i could.
i hope that my knees will still be bruised
from all of the times i fell along the way
but chose to get back up again. i hope
that i can say that i was never too proud
to reach for the hand that held the whole
world but still chose to search for me.
i hope that i praised as much as i pleaded.
i hope that my weaknesses drove me to
further my desire to make something
beautiful from whatever they were meant
to teach me. i hope too, that on that day,
when breath evades my lungs, that i will
have loved to the depths that i was loved.
that i will have forgiven all there was to
forgive, including myself. and i hope with
all my heart that i will leave nothing but
a fresh spring of running water for all
of those who continue to thirst long after
i am gone.

ullie-kaye

my house.

i will surround myself with salty seas
and the incense of sweet deliverance.
i will walk amongst roses; knee high
in petals and blooms and thorns that
ache but do not overtake. i will immerse
my soul in the fragrance of used book
stores and quaint coffee shops and
pavement after rainfall. i will walk on
quiet pathways where the only sound that
lingers is that of my own breath, gasping
at the wonder murmuring all around me.
i will seek for peace in the realms that
are not always visible to the naked eye.
the starlit sky. the winds that sigh.
and i will build my house on this -
i am here for the remainder of my life
and not a moment longer. but i refuse
to let this body perish, while it is yet
meant to live and love and learn its lessons.

ullie-kaye

somewhere to go.

i was full of desert drought and you
did not hesitate to be my rainstorm.
you swept through my darkest and driest
portions and softened the soil of my
spirit. i was empty and you filled me
up with oceans and landscapes and
orchards and made me believe that there
was still harvest left in me. i was tired
and you untangled my feathers one by
one so that i could see what it felt like
to be weightless enough to fly again.
i was lost and you built me a shelter out
of your own marrow and called it "home".
i was haunted by my reflection. you said
i was beautiful. i don't deserve this
kind of love and yet you spoke it into me.
and for whatever it's worth, i still hurt.
but my hurt has somewhere to go.

ullie-kaye

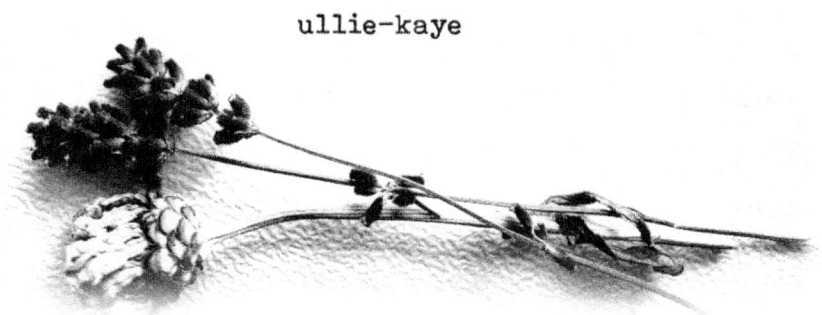

healing.

and on that beautiful morning when
my bones shall return to the earth,
i hope they remember me not only by
my strength but by the weaknesses
that brought me there. i hope they
will talk about my laughter and
how it rang like holy church bells
but understand that it was only by
the grace of my tears that i found
my freedom. i hope too, that on that
day when grief stains their weary
faces, they will know with all their
hearts that healing does not come
when you stop being broken but rather
when your brokenness relinquishes
the power that stops you from healing.

ullie-kaye

full.

may it never be said that i held
onto hurts that needed to be let
go. that i took the road of anger
rather than bathing in the light
of forgiveness. that i chose to
dwell on my misery instead of
fixing my eyes on the beauty of
healing. may it never be said that
i did not love those who the world
considered fallen. or broken.
or different. or unkind. that i did
not extend grace in times when
grace was not easy. may it never
be said that i made myself a
victim of the circumstances rather
than a pillar of endurance. that i
allowed grief to create a prisoner
of me rather than letting it shape
me into someone just a little bit
softer. and braver. and wiser. and
stronger. and may it never be said
that i was ever empty handed.
or empty hearted. or empty anything
at all. i am full, knowing this.
that life is far too short not to
make amends. not to reach for hope.
and not to start again.

ullie-kaye

wonder road.

life gives us so much. the beauty of
slowing down our pace. of turning a
corner. of finding worth and love and
reconnection and grace. life gives us
open doors and open hands and open
hearts. it gives us the opportunity to release.
and learn. and break cycles. life is so
full of collecting small moments and
taking small chances. and finding small
reasons to hold onto faith. it is a long
and winding, wonder road. it is too busy
one moment and too quiet the next.
it teaches us by breaking us. and breaks
us by rearranging us. and rearranges us
into something that is so much better.
and yet, it is just so hard sometimes
to trust that there is something good
in all of this. but my love, there is.
there has to be. we cannot always see
that which we believe in. even the stars
dance in broad daylight when we think
that they are sleeping.

ullie-kaye

soft light.

i just want to be a soft light
in a harsh world. i want my wounds
to serve a purpose. i want my arms
to reach around hurt and hug it away.
i want quiet spaces for rich conversations.
i want more curiosity and less anxiety.
i want doors that swing wide open
and patience for the ones that don't.
i want people to meet me for the very
first time and already know by the
tenderness inside of my eyes that
they can tell me anything.
i just want to be a soft light
in a harsh world.

ullie-kaye

let's be the ones.

let's be the ones who still believe in the art
of moved mountains. in gracious conversations.
in inviting a stranger to tell us their story.
let's be the ones who still gasp at small wonders.
and cheer at small changes. and soak in small
moments. let's carry each other and unburden
each other. and let us never feel that we,
ourselves are too heavy for somebody else to
carry. let's stop pretending and start being okay
with falling apart. and falling together.
let's open our hearts wide enough so that the
ones who are afraid to speak, find their voices.
let's be gentle. and brave. and hopeful.
and let's love like tomorrow isn't a promise.
because it isn't. dear traveler, listen.
time does not always wait for us to get it right.

ullie-kaye

but God.

sometimes when i cannot sleep, i listen
to my heartbeat and remember that i am
still alive. i breathe in and out and watch
as my chest rises and falls with purpose.
sometimes when i cannot sleep, i pretend
that i am a cloud and my bed is the sky
and i drift. and float. and glide. and fly.
and i feel nothing but the softness of not
having to wonder where i am going but rather
resting in how infinitely beautiful the
journey can be. and how i'm surrounded
by love and by angels. and how bravely light
my mind can feel when i give up trying to
be the one who always has to save the world.
because i can't. and i won't. and i'm not
strong enough. but God.

ullie-kaye

86

more than we can handle.

some people will tell you that "God does
not give us more than we can handle",
as though that is a testament to some
extraordinary person we must be to have
been given the honor of such a heavy gift
to carry. the thing is, we ARE given more
than we can hold. a thousand times more.
and sometimes we don't have a choice of
whether we want this to be written into
our story or not. it's hold on or let go.
and it doesn't mean that we are strong.
it means that we are trying to keep every
ounce of our bodies from falling apart.
it's why we must run daily to the shepherd.

ullie-kaye

farewell, old me.

if they ask for the one who cannot
see beyond the thick of the past,
tell them i am no longer here.
if they ask for the one who compares
herself to others, wears herself thin,
tries to fit herself in to spaces that
are too small or too wild or too
shallow for growing.
tell them i have been reborn.
i have left the ocean for the stream.
the darkness for the sun.
i am living simpler. gentler. kinder. softer.
i have gone to make myself more beautiful
in ways that reflect my heart rather
than my body. i am filled with new light.
fresh air. and the kind of peace that
passes understanding. i have started
healing and stopped running.
farewell, old me. i am now free.
i stand before an audience of one.

ullie-kaye

do not make me happy.

do not make me happy.
make me want to string lights upon every
naked tree and see blossoms where they
once hung on like the pink of sky just before
nightfall. make me want to see with eyes
that look through skin and into the deepest
wilds of souls that are beautiful because
they were created. and were created because
they were loved. and were loved because
they were never once an afterthought.
may every blemish in my heart melt to make
room for the ache of others even if it costs me.
open my hands to giving when it isn't comfortable
and receiving when i feel unworthy.
make me want to be eager for healing.
and eager for loving. and eager for wisdom.
let me lap it up like i have been deprived of
water. for days on end. wandering aimlessly.
counting the lonely steps of my own shadow.
do not make me happy. make me want to scatter
a trail of peace wherever i go. telling anyone
who will listen about grace. and freedom.
and that change believes in miracles and miracles
are made of hope and hope is all that we need.
make me want to live like i'm alive and die like
i know where i'm going. do not make me happy.
just make me look for gardens in the graveyards.

ullie-kaye

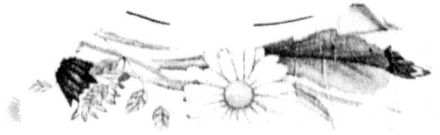

bless you.

bless you for staying gentle.
for picking up the pieces and flying
half-broken. for looking for the stars
in everyone's eyes. even the sad ones.
especially those. bless you for working
through the hard stuff. for waking up
every morning and allowing others to
watch you heal so that they could feel
a little less alone on their journey.
bless you for staying the course.
for carving hope out of grief.
and kindness from emptiness.
bless you for rising above.
for living small.
for choosing your battles even when
you couldn't win them all.
bless you for shining your faith like a
lantern on a hill. like a thousand, glowing
fireflies. like a second chance at grace.
for your willingness to walk alone.
to be misunderstood. and to love anyways.
bless you for that.

ullie-kaye

90

welcome home.

create inner peace.
then you can gather it up and stretch outward
to extend the same peace into every other corner
of your surroundings. because dear soul,
you cannot give what you yourself do not carry.
plant seeds of hope.
then watch how the harvest begins to grow.
how the trees that once wept and withered away,
yield blossoms that spread far and wide and
catch on like fire to paper. oh glory.
love without borders.
then you can find your way through the dark.
because love is the answer. the answer is truth.
and truth is the light. and the light is the way.
it is always the way.
step out in faith.
it's worth it. i promise. the road is not easy and
sometimes you'll fall. but you'll find other people.
you'll stumble together. and somehow you'll
make it. you'll look up and see you were never alone.
you were millions of reasons. you were chosen.
you're home. welcome home.

ullie-kaye

91

forgiveness.

forgiveness looks so good
on you. a fresh spring.
a wildflower in bloom.
green, green grass.
i think it's beautiful how
you have chosen tomorrow
over yesterday.

ullie-kaye

unsaid.

you are so precious. and i think it is truly
tragic if, in all of your years here on this
earth, you were never told. and perhaps you
even began to believe for a moment that the
absence of the words you needed most, meant
that you had no worth. on the contrary.
some have become so hardened that they did not
let the sun shine from their lips. they held
back those landscapes, flowing with trees and
rivers and stars because they did not know how
to speak morning from the nightfall within.
and so they chose rather, to leave things left
unsaid when all the while you craved it so.
and all the while you thought you did not matter.
that these spaces we call days and the distance
we call time and the breaths that kept you here,
were insignificant. but sometimes you need to
become your own curator of love. create it.
nourish it. tend to its fire. keep it burning.
always burning. and as you grow to understand
how beautiful you are, you'll learn to say the
unsaid things to those who need it most -
the ones who never could.

ullie-kaye

connection.

you can crave both solitude and connection.
in fact, i think it is safe to say that those who
live quietly amongst the birds, the seas, the
trees and breezes, simply invite nature in to
spark their inner world. not everyone needs
the noise of city lights to feel alive.
being surrounded and feeling complete and
connected can mean different things to
different people. the soul is only as rich as it
is intertwined with love. and peacekeeping.
and God. essentially, it is not how it comes
but rather, whether it resurrects your spirit.

ullie-kaye

94

refined.

sometimes the most beautiful thing
is the growth that happens after
everything in your life has been
scorched right to the ground.
those tiny, little buds. the sprouts,
bursting wildly. the newness of a
fresh beginning. there is nothing
quite like a life, refined by fire.
that's what i see when i look at you.

ullie-kaye

the wildest parts.

i have heard that real life begins at the end.
that every light that ever spilled its hope onto
earth will join together and shine forever like
stars, holding hands. and i have heard that we
are deeply known. and fiercely loved. and that
sometimes we will lose our way. that darkness
tries to win but won't. and that people do not
always stay. i have heard that our bodies are
spaces that carry our souls. and that every
winter when it gets cold, we grow another layer
of wisdom. i have heard that the rain will tumble
upon us all. that we mustn't believe we are
walking alone. and that angels are breathing
beside us. i have heard that change is good
when it moves your spirit. that the easy part is
not always the best part. and that hearts turn
to gold when they are in the wildest parts of
the fire. this is love. to speak the language of
everlasting things to a world that only knows
the here and now.

ullie-kaye

my little light.

i have a little light that burns,
i try to keep it glowing.
i have to shield it from the winds
that bring along their blowing.
i hold it with my little hands,
although sometimes they're shaking.
i make my way throughout the dark,
the ground beneath me quaking.
i shine it from my little yard,
in hopes it leaps the fences.
onto the grasses, trees and flowers
that permeate my senses.
then on the other side it lands,
'til someone finds it growing
and gathers up a full sized cup
of love that's started flowing.
it spills and builds a little place
where others come to gather.
a little sun, a little moon
and little stars that scatter.
and soon the little light that burns
turns to a sky a blazing
with hopeful, little messengers
that sing of grace, amazing.
so when you think your little light
is too small to unravel,
remember little lights that burn,
find beautiful ways to travel.

ullie-kaye

i behold you.

if beauty is in the eye of the beholder,
then i behold the kindness inside of your soul.
i behold the way you reach around someone
else's hurt and simply listen. i behold your
courage when darkness seeps in. i behold how
you stand at a dead end and look skyward for
directions. i behold how your heart overflows
even when it feels empty and somehow still
makes room to give. i behold the grace with
which you have chosen to carry yourself when
you had every right to grow bitter. i behold the
peace that you have woven out of wilderness.
i behold you. i behold the wonder that you are,
not because of how you were created but because
you are a living, breathing reflection of the
One who created you.

ullie-kaye

the Gardener.

so i shall bloom then.
even with these grieving hands.
my heart half full and half empty.
carried by the wind. warmed by the sun.
drenched in rain. buried in soil.
broken in my waiting. trampled underfoot.
storm on the horizon.
and yet here i am still standing.
and not because i am brave.
not because i am strong.
not because of anything that i have done.
i am small against these breezes after all.
my fragile petals would not stand a chance.
but i was planted here to grow.
and when the Gardener comes along
i want to say with a happy heart,
"i bloomed because you loved me."

ullie-kaye

these tents.

our bodies are just tents.
they are set up on unsteady ground.
they blow like umbrellas bent backwards.
they sit in the heat of the sun until something
is burning. how easily we rupture. burst at the
seams. topple over. untie ourselves from the
little strings that are barely even hanging on.
those grasses that wither and fade.
wither and fade. wither and fade without ending –
oh how we always need some mending.
because our bodies are just tents. but one day,
one day we will be mighty like mountains.
clothed in clouds. held together by the tides
of every ocean. flying with eagles.
bursting with starlight.
we will not come undone by the thread.
we will not tear in the breezes.
we will not crumble with age.
we will not fall into pieces.
we will not wonder at how we shall ever face
the tempest because we will have traded in
our tents for triumph. our holes for hope.
our weeping for worship. our broken strings
for brand new breath. hold on, believer, for
just awhile longer. these tents are not forever.

                    ullie-kaye

you chose.

somewhere along the line, you chose.
you chose to walk the road less traveled.
you chose peace over retaliation.
you chose to take the things that could
have turned your heart cold and became
a light instead. you chose to see the miracles.
you chose to wake up and find goodness.
you chose faith over fear and loved even
when it was not easy.
again and again, you chose.
dear soul, beautiful people are not born.
they are built.

        ullie-kaye

invisible lights.

the best things cannot be seen with eyes.
for at any given time we are being held
together by skies full of otherworldly lights,
flowing in wherever we feel the thick of
darkness upon us. i want you to know that
you are being tended to. that there are
happy whispers even now, of how you shall
be loved. and carried to safety. and led home.
your soul is deep and wide, dear heart.
made with the capacity to grasp the things
that are eternal. beyond the grief of today.
beyond the pain of yesterday. and beyond the
worries of tomorrow. when it hurts the most,
follow the invisible lights. they will always
lead you in the right direction.

ullie-kaye

thankful.

today i am thankful for eyes that
have come to see that life will not
always be easy. that roads will bend.
that lines will blur. that tides will
rise and that storms will come.
i am thankful for those lights that
took the form of human — who shone
into me when i was at my lowest.
who were not afraid of sadness.
or darkness. or the many layers that
wove themselves around me and made me
hard to understand. or reach. or even
hard to love sometimes. i am thankful
for skies that change color. for paths
that change direction. and for seasons
that remind me that we are all just
one breath away from a new beginning.
i am thankful, knowing that kindness
still exists. that the truth is out there.
that faith can move mountains. and that
i was made for every last bit of it.

ullie-kaye

lived.

when you see me, i will look as though
i have lived some years. i will have age
lines and tired eyes. my hair will be
tossed with both windstorms and wisdom.
i will be dressed for comfort rather
than for looks. for warmth rather than
expression. i will have the remnants of
scars that have faded but have not yet
disappeared. i will likely forget a few
words and be holding onto memories just
a little bit tighter than i used to.
but i will be glistening. i will be smiling.
i will be genuinely interested in your life.
i will want to talk about the things that
give you breath and the things that bring
you ache. i will not scurry you away,
for every conversation is an opportunity.
every opportunity is a gift. and every
gift is waiting to be unraveled. and there
is nothing i love more than to watch another
soul find grace. or forgiveness. or a new,
tender way of harvesting light. yes, i have
lived some years. but i have learned the
greatest lessons.

ullie-kaye

light.

there is a certain
kind of light that
only comes from having
been through a certain
kind of darkness.

ullie-kaye

the antidote.

the best medicine you can bring
for sadness is not joy. it is not
telling them that they need to
move on or get over it or realize
how much worse things could be.
no. the medicine for a spirit in
mourning is tenderness. and warmth.
and compassion. and connection.
and presence. sit with someone in
their grief and let them cry their
ugly tears. do not shine and scurry
grief away. they must walk through it.
this is love. to abandon all that we
think we know and be so full of grace
that we are invited in to partake
in someone else's darkest moments.
what an honor it is to simply be a light.
the antidote for sadness is love.
it is always love.

ullie-kaye

hurt and hope.

what if hurt and hope are not so far apart.
what if they are neighbors, sharing a side
yard. living in each other's spaces, under
sunlit skies with tender faces. and what if
hope waters the grasses for hurt and hurt
reminds hope that it's okay to have days
where we feel a little less than prepared to
sip on sun and laughter and all of the delights
around us. what if hurt and hope have a garden.
what if they both tend to the flowers and
caress their petals. hurt knows that the petals
will fall and hope knows that they'll be back
again. when hurt is sick, hope brings the gift
of endurance. when hope is sick, hurt makes
sure to remember that the pathway to hope
requires walking in the dark sometimes.
flashlight on. heavy footsteps. limping to hope's
doorstep and falling down where grace runs
deep. hurt and hope see love with eyes that
shine but know the other side. they welcome
one another in. they weep and smile, they share
a meal and ask each other where they've been.
hurt knows that hope will always stay.
and hope knows that hurt is just a breath away.
they sleep and wake where it's just understood
that hope is kind. but hurt does the spirit good.

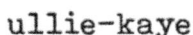

ullie-kaye

107

someplace else.

perhaps not here but someplace else, i am
sitting by a window. curtains, the color of
sunset with seawater, blowing. i am strong
coffee. and bonfire. and harvest moon. full.
and whole. and plenty. loving profusely in all
of the ways that feel like banjos in my hair,
strumming. perhaps not here but someplace
else, my lips are fluent in honoring my body.
in harnessing my inner voice and splattering
it across pavement. and park benches. and
wide, open fields. messy. blatant. chaotic.
unquiet. i drink tides like a sailor who has
seen long days and sleepless nights but
really only ever yearns for home. for rest.
for tenderness. perhaps not here but someplace
else, i am wearing perfume made of long
grasses and wind-soaked trees. these luscious
limbs, laughing. boots made for climbing.
steel-toed and heavy. but light; that ever
flickering light. and here in this place of
otherness, i inhale beauty like my lungs cannot
recognize pain. i am canyon. and cavern. and
canopy. and i do not remember that i have so
far yet to go. because i stay in the moment
of how far i have already come.

ullie-kaye

the ending.

you see, i already know the ending.
good wins. peace prevails. the dragon
is slayed and the sword is raised.
but first we must go through the part
of the story where the plot has not
yet twisted. the battle is not yet won.
the storm is raging. the tower is locked.
the apple is poisoned. the wolf is ready
and waiting in bed, wearing grandmother's
clothing. but i already know the ending.
i already know the ending.

ullie-kaye

joy trickles in.

can joy be found in crumpled hearts,
in empty rooms and broken parts.
can it be found in desert earth,
in washed up dreams and faded worth.
can joy come when the rain outweighs
the happy, blissful, sunny days.
or in the middle of our grief with
words held tight between our teeth.
can joy be found in trembling hands,
where nothing but the unknown stands.
where the unthinkable comes true
and changes everything we knew.
i wonder if joy even knows
how to emerge when sorrow grows.
does it lay down beside the bed
and still caress our weary head.
and is joy really brave enough
to walk along when things get tough.
is joy right there before our eyes
but stuck between our heavy sighs.
i hear joy say that it's okay
to feel both joy and pain today.
whatever loss or lacking light,
joy finds a way to make us bright.
you see our lanterns glow the best
when darkness comes to steal our rest.
and just when sadness seems to win,
joy trickles in.

ullie-kaye

Printed in Great Britain
by Amazon

50074678R00066